A Journal of My Last Week with Mom

PATRICIA DABOH

www.patriciadaboh.com

All scripture quotations are taken from the King James Version of the Holy Bible. Copyright 2012 by Holman Bible Publishers. All Rights Reserved.

A JOURNAL OF YOUR LAST WEEK WITH MOM

You may contact the author at:
patriciadaboh@yahoo.com

ISBN: 978-1-5136-2009-1
Printed in the United States of America

Copyright 2016 by Patricia Daboh

No part of this book may be reproduced or transmitted in any form or by any means, electronic or mechanical, including photocopying, recording, or by any information storage and retrieval system, without permission from the publisher.

Dedications

A Journal of My Last Week with Mom is dedicated to all those who have gone, or are going, through the death journey with a loved one or friend. It's a journey that is filled with emotional highs and lows and one in which we would all bow out of if it were possible — especially the one who is departing this life. The death journey is so immensely surreal that an awakening of priorities and our relationship with God permeates one's mind and lingers there long after our loved one departs. May God strengthen and comfort you during your death journey with your loved one — as he did me during my journey with my dear mother.

This journal is dedicated to my brothers and sisters who tirelessly cared for our mother and never left her side. You were relentless during the storm of cancer. *May God remember your sacrifice of love!*

This journal is dedicated to my children who spoke words of comfort in my soul when I became overwhelmed with tears and sorrow. You traveled back and forth with me from North Carolina to New Jersey to be with mom. You prayed with me and for me. *Thank you so very much!*

This journal is dedicated to my mother's pastor, Bishop Edgar D. Robinson of Christ Gospel Love Center Church in Whitesboro, New Jersey. You fed mom the word of God for years, cherished her, and loved her in every season of her life. I greatly appreciate you and your church family being there for mom. *Thank you!*

This journal is dedicated to Evangel Fellowship, my church family in Greensboro, North Carolina. You reached out to me when I was with mom during her hospice care, and it comforted me greatly. *Thank you!*

Last, but not least, this journal is dedicated to my dear mother, **Audrey Lydia Carolyn Hicks Smith**, who departed this life on Wednesday, June 22, 2016. "Even during your transition to heaven, mom, you did it with dignity, calmness, and the blessed assurance that the Lord Jesus never left your side. You showed your children that it is possible to transition from this earthly life to heaven in a peaceful state of mind — not begrudging God's timing--even if you did not want to go. *You were brave, mom, and you held onto your faith. I love you!"*

CONTENTS

Dedications

Introduction: March 2016.............................. 1

1. Saturday, June 18, 2016...................4

2. Sunday, June 19, 2016 20

3. Monday, June 20, 2016 24

4. Tuesday, June 21, 2016 30

5. Wednesday, June 22, 2016 38

6. When God Speaks 44

7. Afterword 46

8. Forever in My Heart........................50

Introduction

March 2016

When my phone rang, I immediately remembered I hadn't returned my sister's call from earlier this morning. In thinking about our conversation after the call ended, I realized my sister chose to share the grave news with me in the evening — wanting to postpone the emotional pain she knew would grip my heart. My sister asked me if I was free to talk, and I let her know I was after apologizing for forgetting to call her back when I got off work. She said, "Mom got the results of her tests, and she has bilateral lung cancer!" The silence on the phone grew longer between us as I struggled to accept what she just said. In that moment, I thought about the medical challenges mom has been through in her life, and now she has cancer. I wanted my voice to sound strong and confident when I spoke, but instead I heard the uncertainty and shock reflected in my response as I said, "You mean it's in both lungs?"

"Yes", my sister said, "it's in both of her lungs", and the silence on the phone grew longer this time. I searched my memory for promises I believe God shared with me concerning mom, and I remembered I had a dream some time ago that mom lived to see her 100th birthday. The dream was so vivid and real, and I believed it was a revelation that mom would indeed live to see her 100th birthday. The same week I had the dream, mom told me she asked God to allow her to live to 100 years old. We were both delighted and overjoyed—believing the timing of my dream and her prayer request was a confirmation that God was going to grant her the desire of her heart. These thoughts were sailing through my mind as my sister waited patiently on the other end of the phone for me to say something further. "I had a dream that mom lived until she was 100 years old, and I'm just crazy enough to believe God can do anything", I said with that same uncertainty in my voice.

Just then my niece said something, and I realized my sister and her daughter were both waiting for my response together. I don't remember what was said after that point; but when I hung up the phone, I felt confused as to why mom had cancer when I dreamed she was going to live to 100 years old. I was upset that she had to deal with yet another medical condition after all she has been through.

The next day, mom and I talked about her prayer and my dream, and I encouraged her to believe God — regardless of the news she received from her doctor. From that moment on, I became mom's spiritual cheerleader and encourager! I assured her the doctor's report was not the final authority, but we would believe God for a complete healing. Because of my dream, I felt assured mom would beat cancer — we both believed she would!

Saturday, June 18, 2016

Standing in front of mom's china cabinet admiring everything she had placed in it over the years, I glanced back at her sleeping in an upward position on the couch. She sleeps mostly all day now and eats and drinks very little. There is such a significant difference in her health from when my daughter, my grandson and I visited her two weeks ago. During that visit, she was at least eating three small meals a day. She watched her favorite gospel show on the television and enjoyed having the bible read to her by my younger sister.

Night Watch

Wanting to give my siblings a break, I volunteered to stay with mom around-the-clock during my second visit with her in June. Sometimes she tries to scoot to the edge of the couch at night and raises her arms high above her head — like a child does who wants to be picked up by a parent.

Perhaps mom is motioning for God to come and deliver her from the cancerous battle she is fighting. She sometimes engages in conversations with people only she can see while she slumbers, and she sometimes moves her hands around rapidly as if she were searching for something.

I moved over closer to mom who is sleeping on one end of the couch and placed the cover back over her. Rather than sleep in her bedroom, she prefers to sleep in an upward position on the couch—using pillows to cushion her head comfortably. She opens her mouth wide with each breath—indicating the oxygen flowing through the tube and into her nostrils isn't giving her sufficient air flow—although the machine is turned up to the highest level. It is emotionally disturbing, watching mom struggle to breathe. *"Lord, I want mom to get better"*, I pleaded with each breath she took. I watch the rise and fall of her chest—hoping it continues to do so.

As mom sleeps, I journal. Journaling my experience helps me release the bottled-up emotions that I cannot openly express as I care for her. At times, I feel like screaming, kicking, and rolling on the floor like a child who is having a temper tantrum and wants something. *"Stop her suffering, Lord!"*, I want to say. Yet, outwardly, I am calm, soothing and encouraging. Oh, what conflicting emotions one endures when experiencing the death journey with a loved one.

Hospice Care

After several radiation treatments and one chemo drip, it was obvious that mom was not improving. If she survived her battle with cancer, it would be done by God's intervention — not mankind. Her oncologists were realistic about the probability of her recovering from the onset of her diagnosis due to her having multiple health conditions — combined with her age.

It was even suggested by one of them that some people choose to not take any treatment and spend the remainder of their time with their family. However, mom has always been a fighter, and she wanted to use whatever available medical interventions there were that could possibly keep her alive and improve her chances for a quality life.

More tests revealed the cancer had spread to her bones, stomach and liver. The tumor in her stomach was large enough that she could feel it through her skin. She would sometimes place her hand over her stomach tumor — seemingly amazed that this was now part of her body. Her oncologists wanted to do another test to determine if the cancer spread to her brain, but mom had enough of tests that could possibly reveal more dismal news. She never consented to that test.

The day before I returned to New Jersey for the second time in June, it was decided that mom would be sent home on hospice care. Mom had grown tired of medical interventions that were not rewarded with improved health. The interrupted hospital sleep was taking its toll on her, and she was weary. Mom was being settled in at home when I returned during my second visit.

Emotional Roller Coaster

Earlier today I tried to encourage mom to take a sip of water, for she had taken only a few sips all day. She was reluctant to drink some water at first, so I began singing an impromptu song, *"Please momma take a sip of water"*, as I danced around in front of her hoping to make her smile. I was rewarded with a beautiful smile, as she rolled her eyes up and said, "*Ok, Patricia, I'll take a sip since you keep bothering me*".

I looked down at her thin face and lifted the bottle of water to her lips. She took one big gulp, smiled again and said, "*Are you happy now*"? "*Yes*", I said rather sassily, delighted she at least tried. I realized, though, she took that sip of water for my comfort of mind — not because she wanted it. Cancer is a horrific disease — rendering its recipients with the loss of one's appetite and stripping away the ability to do the simple things in life we take for granted.

Before I visited mom for the second time, I prayed and asked God to either heal mom or take her to heaven to be with him. It is very painful watching mom suffer the effects of cancer. During this second visit, I took a week of unplanned and unpaid leave from work. When a loved one is seriously ill, the battle to balance paying the bills and taking as much PTO leave that is possible without losing your job can get frustrating and complicated. Even though a loved one is on a journey that may be ending, the realities of life still loom ever so big for the caregivers. When mom was placed under hospice care, I knew this would be my last visit with her unless I resigned my position. Having accepted a new position just seven months ago, I didn't meet the requirements for a job absence/security under the Family Medical Leave Act. Just imagining mom not eating, not drinking and dwindling away many miles from me is too painful to think about. I realized during my first day back with mom, that my prayer for God to either heal her or take her to heaven was somewhat selfish. I was trying to spare my agony of watching her suffer. I was trying to spare my pain and my discomfort of being separated from her as she possibly dies. I imagined how frightened she must feel after being told she has bilateral lung cancer, bone cancer, stomach cancer and liver cancer.

Yet, she is bravely facing what is happening to her—wanting to comfort her children as we take care of her. Isn't it amazing how mothers protect us even as we become adults? That protective motherhood instinct never grows old with time.

Acceptance

Even though mom understood what hospice care meant and accepted the fact that she needed it, glimpses of the hope of her recovering would spring forth like sunshine after a heavy rain. I overheard mom talking to my sister. She asked her if they could do anything for her at the hospital, and my sister told her they've done everything they can at this point. Mom said, "Then what will happen to me"? My sister said, "You'll die mom if you don't get better". The room fell silent. No more words were said. It was as if mom was beginning to accept the possibility that she may die, for she was not getting better. That was a difficult realization to come to terms with — especially since mom was active just a few months ago.

Mom's Glory Days

Mom went to church on Sundays and attended bible study on Tuesdays. She went to a senior center twice a week and participated in its activities. She went three times a week when they had a special program. Mom made friends easily in the newly built senior center where she resided, and she often met her friends in the activity room where they played bingo and cards for non-monetary gifts. She organized and oversaw a weekly prayer session for those who wanted to pray collectively for others. She founded a prosthetic group and met with them once a month at the local hospital--having experienced an amputation below the right knee several years ago due to diabetes. She served as a board member of *Fare Free*, which offers transportation to those who need it. She sent cards and telephoned church members and friends when they were sick. She also visited those who were ill-- encouraging them and helping them as much as her health conditions would allow. She engaged in family gatherings with her children, grandchildren and great grandchildren on numerous occasions--enjoying the meals and conversations that flowed freely.

We're Not Ready

To go from such an active lifestyle to not being able to bathe yourself, not being able to walk to the bathroom to use it, not being able to prepare your own food, not being able to hold your bible to read its passages, and not being able to catch your breath with the slightest movement is heartbreaking and frightening. Mom isn't ready to leave, and we aren't ready for her to go. Watching her downward spiral is at times almost unbearable! Sometimes I feel like I'm the one dying as I watch her fight her battle with cancer.

When I am feeling overwhelmed with emotional pain, God comforts me--as I know he is comforting mom while she's walking through the valley of the shadow of death. As a child, I would sometimes try to catch my shadow on the sidewalk on a sunny day. This journey with mom feels like the shadow of death is chasing her, and she is attempting to elude its grasp--but it's gaining on her. When a loved one is dying, we realize our humanity ever so profoundly.

My sister and I were sitting in mom's living room and looking around. It was as if with each glance around the room, we were seeing what was important and dear to her. My sister said, *"It's like these things are not even hers anymore"*. I understood what she meant, for mom was so ill that she could not connect with anything she had acquired over the years. The wall decorations no longer could be admired by her, the place where the light beamed through the blinds to brighten her day where she usually sat putting a puzzle together was vacant, and the television that broadcasted her favorite gospel shows was silent. The realization of her impending transition was constantly looming there and preparing our hearts and minds for what was to come. Mom was traveling to another realm where tangible items have no value or meaning. It's in those moments that we realize even more that the intangible choices we make throughout life are what is important and what will sustain us through our journey from earth to heaven. We're just pilgrims journeying through this land, for our human bodies weren't created to dwell on this side forever.

When Comfort Is All You Have

I just glanced back at mom again, and she's still sleeping. She woke up for a moment saying she was concerned that her leg was weak and how sad it is that she can't walk anymore. I reached for her hand and stroked it letting her feel the warmth of my comfort and love. *"It's alright, mom"*, I assured her as she drifted back off to sleep.

When Mom woke up again, she said she wanted to go to church tomorrow. The last time she tried to go to church, she was rushed to the hospital. *"Bless you mom, for you're still trying"*, I whispered inwardly as I watched her drift right back off to sleep. *"I love you!"*

God Whispered

I heard God whisper "Tuesday" in my spirit, and I later told my siblings that day will be significant. I pray Tuesday is mom's healing date — not her heavenly transition date.

Preparation for Church

Before mom got settled down on the couch tonight, my sister gave her a sponge-bath for church tomorrow. Although we felt she was too sick to go to church, mom wanted to go. Not knowing whether this would be her last church service — and against our better judgment — we gave into her request.

Sleepless Night

At first, mom got winded when she walked. Then, mom got winded at the slightest movement—such as fumbling through her pocketbook for a sugar-free mint. Now, mom gets winded just sitting still. Watching mom sleep reminds me of when I gave birth to my oldest child and brought her home from the hospital. I watched the rise and fall of my daughter's chest--making sure my newborn baby was breathing. Watching a loved one struggle to breathe with lung cancer requires vigilant stamina, and it is accompanied with a floodgate of conflicting thoughts and emotions as your companion. On one hand, you're praying to God for total restoration; and on the other hand, you want your loved one's suffering to be over. I watch mom as she takes each breath--hoping it won't be her last. She wakes up quite often speaking words that are incoherent.

Our First Visit

During our first visit, mom began engaging in conversations with other people that were not visible to our human eye. We weren't quite sure whether her visions were coming from the effects of the round-the-clock narcotics she was taking to control her pain, or if she was actually seeing others that had gone on before her — and she was preparing to trade her cancer diseased body for one that would never feel pain again. All I know is that I want our present circumstance to do a 360-degree shift and for mom to feel well again.

Sunday, June 19, 2016

It's 2:41 am, and I am still watching mom breathe. I purposely came to spend every moment of our precious week together — never leaving her side. I find it amazing how emotional pain can coincide right beside faith--the one battling the other for supremacy — so that one can scream the victor. During my chest watching vigil, faith claimed the victory. *"Mom will live"*, I proclaimed inwardly — convincing myself and forcing my faith to look beyond what my human eyes were seeing to a place of peace and happy endings. However, when mom's breathing indicated a less than normal rhythm, stabbing pains broke through the facade of my strength as emotions invaded me like a flood. "Jesus, be my strength and strong tower. Rise up in me as I take my watch over mom in the wee hours of this Sunday morning", I prayed silently.

My chest felt so full of emotions, but I dared not allow one tear drop to escape—lest mom awaken and see my emotional state. *"It's not about me, but it's about supporting mom"*, I told myself.

Psalm 23

Mom just reached for my hand, and her fingers feel cold. The coldness of her hands made me think about Psalm 23.

"The Lord is my shepherd; I shall not want.

He maketh me to lie down in green pastures: he leadeth me beside the still waters.

He restoreth my soul: he leadeth me in the paths of righteousness for his name's sake.

Yea, though I walk through the valley of the shadow of death, I will fear no evil: for thou art with me; thy rod and thy staff they comfort me.

Thou preparest a table before me in the presence of mine enemies: thou anointest my head with oil; my cup runneth over.

Surely goodness and mercy shall follow me all the days of my life: and I will dwell in the house of the Lord forever."

It feels as though we are all walking through the valley of the shadow of death when a loved one is fighting a deadly disease—yet God is with us. He's comforting us. Cancer is horrific! We must find a cure. *"Lord, please give us the knowledge to eradicate cancer's ravishing effects on mankind"*, I prayed softly in the air. *"Perhaps I'll close my eyes for just a few minutes"*, I thought a second ago. I feel so sleep deprived that it seems to be my normal state now, yet I don't want to miss one second with mom.

Church Meltdown

I hoped mom's church experience would lift her far above her present cancer diagnosis. Rather than that happening, we almost loss mom right at church.

After arriving somewhat late at church, mom's oxygen tank ran out too soon; and one of the portable tanks didn't work properly! As some of the church members, who are nurses, ran over to help us, we rushed mom out of the sanctuary into the hallway. I literally had a *"melt down"* of tears as each second ticked by without mom receiving the precious oxygen she needed to breathe. My older sister comforted me as the saints laid hands on mom praying to keep her calm and focused on Jesus—rather than the situation. We all rejoiced when the oxygen began to flow and mom was able to breathe again. However, due to her experience at church, mom slept many hours when we got her home.

On Sunday afternoon, all of my siblings gathered in mom's living room talking casually as we watched her chest rise and fall. I hope it will not be her last day with us.

Monday, June 20, 2016

Monday was the best day with mom, for she was more alert and ate a little without much coaxing. Mom even threw in some light humor when engaging in conversation. *"Go momma"*, I rejoiced inwardly as I hoped the healing power of God would transform her back to her former self.

We moved mom from her favorite spot on the couch back into her bedroom, for her foot started swelling. It was obvious mom had to elevate her foot—although she did not like to be in her bedroom. Using many pillows, we propped her up in a sitting position in the middle of her bed; and I sat at the foot of her bed attempting to put together a 500-piece puzzle that had previously been completed by mom and then taken apart again and placed back in its box.

I wanted to show mom I was going to continue with one of her favorite past-times. I'd never shown any inclination toward completing puzzles in the past, but I was determined to learn. I placed the puzzle pieces on a large cardboard at the bottom of mom's bed and picked out the edge pieces—having been instructed by mom to put the outside of the puzzle together first. I played mom's favorite old school, gospel songs she loves so very much. The songs flowed through the air and through our souls as we settled down into the roles of master puzzle maker and puzzle student. Mom mouthed the words of the songs—with no sounds coming from her to reserve her precious oxygen. During my last visit, though, mom and I sang song-after-song glorifying God and filling her home with soulful, gospel tunes. She was more awake, than asleep, during that visit; and she could breathe better.

As I was putting a puzzle piece in its place, I looked up to see mom staring at me. She said very softly, *"You're very patient, and I appreciate you loving me and caring for me"*. Before I could respond, she drifted off to sleep. I found her gratefulness amazing, for she was my dear mother. Where else would I, or my siblings, be at a time like this than by her side.

Later that day, my youngest brother, his wife, and my sister-in-law's aunt came by to see mom. Mom was surprisingly alert this afternoon—more than usual. We all crowded into her bedroom conversing about various subjects and enjoying one another's company. Mom said, *"Let's go in the living room, for life is in there"*. Thinking about her comment later, I believe she was associating health with the absence of a bed, nebulizer, and oxygen machine which was part of her bedroom décor now. My brother picked mom up, put her in her transport wheelchair and pushed her into the living room with us. The conversation picked up in the living room as though it had never stopped. She looked happy and glad for the change of scenery. Mom stayed up with us late into the evening--only taking brief naps. I thought she just might beat cancer! We all remarked how good mom looked and did today. Life for the moment seemed almost normal. We were all encouraged on today.

Tonight, mom slept in her bed. While glancing at mom sleeping, I remembered reading the words of a world-famous gospel minister. He said, *"before his mother died, she seemed to improve"*. I don't know why that thought crept in my mind like an unwanted fog after a heavy rain, but nevertheless, I found myself wondering if this was mom's "good day" before she died. I began thanking God for the bountiful blessing of seeing mom in her "almost glory state" where her physical discomfort seemed improved.

"Yes", I whispered in the air, *"I am going to dwell on the positive. Let tomorrow take care of itself when that time comes. For now, Lord Jesus, I thank you for blessing her to be surrounded by her family and taking part in simple conversations, which brought all of us immense joy!"*

Weariness

I laid on the couch in the dark — not wanting to fall asleep for fear I would not check on mom enough throughout the night. I felt strange being separated from mom, for I had grown accustomed to drifting in and out of sleep in a sitting position on the couch. When a loved one is fighting a life-threatening disease, you are affected by emotions — positive and negative ones — and the weariness of one's soul can feel so overwhelming that words alone cannot adequately describe it. My mind, although dulled due to the lack of sleep, continued to function like a well-oiled machine — keeping me awake. I jumped up several times throughout the night checking on mom, watching her breathe and praying for a miracle!

Tuesday, June 21, 2016

As my sister watched mom this morning, I walked across the busy Bayshore Road in North Cape May, New Jersey to Uncle Bill's Restaurant—one of my mother's favorite restaurants. The restaurant was popular with both residents and vacationers for serving delicious breakfast platters. As I neared Uncle Bills, a burst of sadness exploded in my heart—and I fought to hold back the tears that threatened to fall and expose my sorrow. Mom seemed to have slipped back to her former state this morning. She was laying all the way down on her bed this morning, which was a rare thing for her to do. She slept deeply and did not wake to drink nor eat. As I walked across the street, I thought about mom not having an appetite to eat or drink this morning—laying on her bed possibly slipping away from us.

"Lord Jesus", I cried inwardly as I kept walking, *"Please don't let my mother die today. Life would not be the same without her in this world--in my world!"*

The Storm Early Tuesday Morning
Before Dawn

My Tuesday had already started off much more adventurous than I would have preferred this morning. While sleeping on the couch in mom's living room, I was awakened suddenly by a loud bang early Tuesday morning before dawn! The noise was so deafening that I jumped up, lost my footing and fell on the floor — hurting both knees in the process. I felt disoriented about what was happening. I thought mom had fallen out of bed, for she did not want a hospital bed — preferring rather to sleep in her familiar one. I yelled out, "I'm coming, Mom", as I jumped up from the floor and took off running towards mom's bedroom. At that moment, the electricity went out, and I exclaimed, *"Jesus help us!"* I heard the thunder roaring and frantically felt on the kitchen counter for my cell phone, so I could use its flashlight to see.

In the darkness, I heard mom's oxygen machine slowing down until it finally shut off, and I cried out again, *"Jesus, please help us"!* Mom was still sleeping, so she didn't realize her oxygen machine stopped working. However, she must have heard me groping around in the dark and whispered, *"What's wrong".* I said, *"Everything is alright",* not wanting her to panic if she realized her oxygen machine was no longer on. About 20 seconds later—the rhythm of mom's oxygen machine began in motion again—and it was the sweetest sound I'd ever heard! *"Thank you, Jesus"*, I rejoiced out loud as I praised God for sparing mom's life and my sorrow.

Just then the building maintenance man knocked on the door and informed me that the activity room down the hall had a back-up generator. He wanted to run a long extension cord from mom's oxygen machine to that room in case the electricity went out again during the storm. The cord was plugged into mom's machine, run down the hallway and plugged into an electric socket in the activity room. Within a few minutes, the electricity went back out again. It seemed as if the enemy was fighting against us in the early hours of Tuesday morning, but God gave us the victory! The scripture in Isaiah 54:17, *"No weapon that is formed against thee shall prosper"*, came to mind.

I discovered later that a tornado touched down a few blocks from mom's place and knocked out the electricity in her area. By late Tuesday morning, the electricity was restored on mom's block—although the surrounding blocks were still without power.

Mom's Downward Spiral

When I came back from Uncle Bill's Restaurant, I began to realize the joy we felt on Monday was short-lived, for mom seem to take a turn for the worse. I used my smartphone to google the signs and symptoms of death, and I realized mom may be dying soon. Her left foot (her right leg had been amputated below the knee some years ago) had been swollen for a few days and was now "cold" to the touch. The coldness was spreading to her ankle and up her leg. Her fingers were also cold. Rather than sleep propped up in her usual sitting position, she laid down flat on her pillow in her bed. *"Dear, Jesus"*, I whispered in my heart, *"It seems as if momma is slipping away"!*

Mom's Last Night with Us

Later tonight, my aunt and cousin came to visit mom. I was glad to see them, for I hadn't seen them in a long time. I let my sister know they were here to see mom, and asked them to wait a few minutes before going in her bedroom. I heard mom moan out in pain, and I believed she must have asked my sister to prop her up in a sitting position using her pillows to receive her visitors. I also knew it was difficult for her to be propped up right now, for we noticed she was developing a bed sore — despite our best efforts to keep that from happening. Although mom was in pain and it was difficult for her to breathe, she was glad to see them. During their visit, mom kept dozing off to sleep; and at one point my aunt excused herself to have a silent cry in the living room — realizing her sister was extremely ill and may be slipping away.

After my cousin left, mom appeared to get weaker and weaker by the minute. She reached for my hand, and I took it gently in mine and stood next to her bedside for a long time holding onto her. She wanted to lean on me and not be placed back in her resting place in the middle of her bed. At this point, mom did not speak. Perhaps she knew she was slipping away. I wanted to move her over further in the middle of the bed to make her more comfortable, but she did not want to move over. I called a few of my siblings to help me talk mom into being placed back in the middle of her bed where she would not be in danger of toppling forward. I saw the mental shift when she was finally ready to move over in the bed. Her shoulders rose and fell in resolution as she inhaled and exhaled a breath and whispered, *"I'm ready now"*. I lifted mom gently and positioned her further in the middle of her bed, and her breath was very short from the exertion.

"Just a little further, and you will be far enough over in the bed", I told her as she was catching her breath from being moved over the first time. At that moment, my older sister walked through the door and assisted in placing mom in what would become her final resting place on her bed. From this point on, mom never opened her eyes again or said another word.

Mom's Transition to Heaven
Wednesday, June 22, 2016

My older sister decided to spend the night, and my aunt was staying for a few days. Mom's one-bedroom apartment was not able to accommodate many people. Therefore, my aunt slept on the couch, my sister slept on the floor in the living room, and I slept in mom's rocking chair in the living room. Around 2:30 a.m., I awakened stiff from sleeping in the rocking chair and decided, rather, to sleep in mom's bedroom on the floor. Because of where mom's oxygen machine was located, I decided to sleep on the floor between the foot of mom's bed and her dresser. Before laying on the floor, I looked at mom leaning back against her pillows. Her mouth was opening wider than before, and she was taking in much deeper breaths.

Watching her breathe so heavy was distressful, but I was glad she was still breathing. After watching her for a while, I settled down on the floor and fell asleep feeling totally exhausted. When I awakened a few hours later, I laid still on the floor before moving—hoping to hear the erratic rhythm of her heavy breathing. After listening for a few minutes, I sat up and looked at her. Nothing had changed. Mom was still propped up against her pillows breathing heavily through her mouth. A week ago, mom decided that she did not want to have tubes placed down her throat to keep her breathing if she was unable to breathe on her own. As difficult as that decision was for mom to make and for us (*her children*) to accept, we respected her by honoring her wishes. Mom was fighting four types of cancers, and she was tired. She had been given many radiation treatments and one chemo treatment, yet her condition had not improved.

Mom was simply tired of machines, tired of sleep-induced narcotics and tired of constantly struggling to capture oxygen in her deprived lungs. Her quality of life had diminished so greatly at this point. She was simply tired!

I laid back down on the floor and fell asleep again. When I awakened, I again laid still at first and listened for the rhythm of her breathing. This time, however, I heard only the hissing sound of oxygen flowing through the tube — hitting against her nostrils. I jumped up and hurried to her side. She was no longer propped up in a sitting position, but she had slid much further down on her pillows flat on her back. Her arms were raised and resting next to both sides of her head, and her hands were in a curled-up position. Her body posture looked as if she had accepted and surrendered to her fate! Her face was tilted toward the wall, and her eyes were half-way open and glassed over — indicating her life was almost over.

The oxygen continued to hiss against her nostrils, which no longer would need it in a few minutes. Her stomach rose high and settled back down with great effort. I ran in the living room and roused my sister who was still sleeping on the floor and let her know mom was almost gone at this point. My sister walked briskly in her bedroom and began rubbing mom's arm. As she rubbed her arm, mom's stomach rose again and fell one last time. During these last few minutes of her life — she never opened her mouth for oxygen — and her eyes remained transfixed as if she were already gone. We stood and looked at her for a while before waking my aunt to tell her that her last remaining sister was gone.

    Hospice had already prepared us about what to do when mom passed away, and we called them. They would have to come to the house and pronounce her dead.

I had never seen a loved one die before, but God answered my prayer *"to either heal her or take her to heaven"*. Towards the end of mom's life, she would speak out, unaware that she did, asking God *"how long do I have to be in the wilderness"?* When God took mom, he answered both of our prayers. **Her suffering was now over!**

Although my mother and I were separated by distance, we were close in relationship. We loved one another. We talked several times on the phone daily. We both cherished our relationship with the Lord Jesus and talked many times about becoming what the Lord would have us to be. I stood there looking down at my mother's lifeless body feeling sad that she had not recovered — but instead she was gone from us! Upon hearing the initial diagnosis three months ago, I really believed she would beat this cancerous disease and be healed.

Neither mom's desire to live to celebrate her 100th birthday nor my dream that she did, was realized. Yet, God is still good! Can God not do what he wants with what he created? Yes, he can!

When God Speaks

While driving back to mom's apartment after attending the private family viewing at the funeral home, I continued my daily talk with God about how much I missed mom and thought she would be healed. When I pulled up to a red light, God whispered to my soul ever so gently, **"Count Your Blessings"**. My entire perspective changed in that moment! Many people have not had a mother who loved and adored them, met their needs, and sacrificed their personal desires in life for the betterment of their children as long as I have had. Rather than continue my whining about why my mom died, I began to acknowledge God's blessings in my life and praised him for the time I had with my dear mother on earth. *"Isn't God good to not allow me to continue in a habitual, torturous mental exercise of asking him why mom died over-and-over again. God answered my question by simply speaking three little words,* **"Count Your Blessings!"**

God allowed me to be with mom during her last week on earth and when she transitioned to heaven—and by doing so he answered my prayer. Those three words have allowed me to refocus from whining to praise. God is good—even when the answer to our prayer is "no".

3 Blessed be God, even the Father of our Lord Jesus Christ, the Father of mercies, and the God of all comfort;

4 Who comforteth us in all our tribulation, that we may be able to comfort them which are in any trouble, by the comfort wherewith we ourselves are comforted of God."

2 Corinthians 1:3-4

Afterword

So now my journey begins without my mother. I wonder how young children cope with the loss of a parent, guardian or loved one; for it is difficult for me to deal with as an adult. Although I no longer whine about mom dying, there are times I cry simply because I miss her. I was accustomed to hearing her voice. I was accustomed to hearing what she did each day. I was accustomed to knowing what she ate each day. I was accustomed to knowing how she felt. I was accustomed to hearing the cleverness with which she conversed so freely. *I was accustomed to her each day!* When mom died, it felt like my hands were full of her and then they were abruptly emptied. Yet, good has come out of mom's death. I am determined to love more deeply each day. I am determined to forgive more quickly. I am determined to allow God to transform my life for his glory, kingdom and honor each day.

Watching my dear mother pass through the death journey has changed my life forever! Regardless of what we accumulate in this life, it is of small significance as we are departing this world. Our possessions (cars, homes, assets, clothes, shoes, and money etc.) cannot be enjoyed on the death journey. These seemingly, important tangible items are then categorized as being insignificant as compared to our relationship with God, family and mankind. Seeing death up close and personal — as I have seen as I watched my dear mother transition to her heavenly destination — has deepened my commitment to Jesus Christ and his will for my life. I truly see and understand that o*nly what we do for Christ will last!*

Mom never got angry with God when she was dying—rather she called on him even more. She did not want to die, but she understood that decision was not hers to make, but it belonged to God. I'm so glad my dear mother loved the Lord Jesus, and she lived for him until she took her last breath. I'm glad the Lord blessed me to be with my dear mother during the last week of her life. It's comforting picturing mom in God's presence free from disease and pain. Sometimes the only way to press beyond the painful memories of how cancer ravished and affected her body during her last week on earth, is to picture her in heaven with the Lord Jesus. Those memories become bearable then.

"Mom, even on your death journey you taught your children a lesson. We love you, Mom!"

⁵³ For this corruptible must put on incorruption, and this mortal must put on immortality.

⁵⁴ So when this corruptible shall have put on incorruption, and this mortal shall have put on immortality, then shall be brought to pass the saying that is written, **Death is swallowed up in victory***.*

⁵⁵ O death, where is thy sting? O grave where is thy victory?

1 Corinthians 15:53-55

A Journal of My Last Week with Mom

Forever in My Heart

I miss hearing your voice
It was a delight each day.
I miss seeing your smile
That brought sunshine my way.

I miss feeling your comfort
And the love you had for me.
Those precious, beautiful moments
That now can never be.

Yet in the stillness of your absence
You're here within my heart.
And I shall always love you
Even though we are apart.

"Rest in Jesus, Mom!"

Patricia Daboh

Made in the USA
Middletown, DE
10 May 2017